WHOLENESS

Powerful Journal Meditations for Inner Healing

TENEKA G. MILES

It is a joy to share this journal with you. It is a compilation of meditations and heart-opening scriptures gathered throughout my journey of longing for WHOLENESS. This journey was often filled with feelings of abandonment, rejection, shame, fear, unworthiness, and emptiness until my heart opened and embraced this infinite presence of Love we call God. My prayer is that through these meditations your heart will be filled with such joy and peace and you, too, will know and experience WHOLENESS.

Blessings and Peace,
Teneka

Our actions can be so undeserving of mercy, yet the Love of God outweighs our futile attempts to live a life that can only be lived by utterly depending upon Him and His Amazing grace. True freedom is in recognizing our need for Him.

_____

_____

_____

_____

_____

_____

_____

_____

_____

_____

_____

_____

_____

_____

_____

_____

_____

_____

_____

For with You is the fountain of life; in Your light do we see light **(Psalm 36:9)**

We are not always where we WANT to be; but we are usually where we NEED to be. Lean into the moment, space, or time that you wish to escape or avoid. Ask God what must you learn to pass through your seasons with joy and gratitude!!!!

_____

_____

_____

_____

_____

_____

_____

_____

_____

_____

_____

_____

_____

_____

_____

_____

_____

_____

_____

_____

My God, I trust, lean on, rely on, and am confident in You. Let me not be put to shame or [my hope in You] be disappointed; let not my enemies triumph over me **(Psalm 25:2)**

Trust the Father to lead you by his Spirit into and unto all truth. May all that is hidden be uncovered before your eyes. May that which you need to know be revealed and may peace follow your decisions.

_____

_____

_____

_____

_____

_____

_____

_____

_____

_____

_____

_____

_____

_____

_____

_____

_____

_____

_____

As for me, I will continue beholding Your face in righteousness (rightness, justice, and right standing with You); I shall be fully satisfied, when I awake to find myself beholding Your form and having sweet communion with You **(Psalm 17:15)**.

Waiting on someone else to make you happy is the best way to be sad. We must never wait on the actions of others for outcomes we control.

_____

_____

_____

_____

_____

_____

_____

_____

_____

_____

_____

_____

_____

_____

_____

_____

_____

_____

_____

_____

_____

_____

_____

And now, Lord, what do I wait for and expect? My hope and expectation are in You **(Psalm 39:7)**

Just agree with God! Resisting his direction only leads to frustration and disappointment. Learn to yield to the unseen divine guidance in your life. Your Father leads you in the direction of peace and righteousness no matter what the appearance of the journey maybe. Just let go and TRUST!

_____

_____

_____

_____

_____

_____

_____

_____

_____

_____

_____

_____

_____

_____

_____

_____

_____

_____

_____

_____

Then will I go to the altar of God, to God, my exceeding joy; yes, with the instruments will I praise You, O God, my God **(Psalm 43:4)**

Life is but a vapor! Please don't spend ONE MORE moment with an ungrateful heart. Embrace and enjoy every breath that is granted to you. Stop and discern the abundance that is bestowed upon you.

_____

_____

_____

_____

_____

_____

_____

_____

_____

_____

_____

_____

_____

_____

_____

_____

_____

_____

_____

_____

In Your name they rejoice all the day, and in Your righteousness they are exalted **(Psalm 89:16)**

True contentment is not in the attainment of that which you believe will bring you contentment (love, prosperity, people, stuff, etc.); rather it is in you recognizing you don't lack the essence of that which you seek. The moment we recognize our WHOLENESS is the moment we experience true contentment with who we are, where we are, and where we are going.

_____

_____

_____

_____

_____

_____

_____

_____

_____

_____

_____

_____

_____

_____

_____

_____

_____

_____

Let the words of my mouth, and the meditation of my heart, be acceptable in thy sight, O LORD, my strength, and my redeemer **(Psalm 19:14)**

Where humility is needed, self-righteousness is often present. Life is much more peaceful when we let go of our need to be heard and to be right. There is but ONE who is true and right. The rest of us are products of His love and grace.

_____

_____

_____

_____

_____

_____

_____

_____

_____

_____

_____

_____

_____

_____

_____

_____

_____

_____

_____

He is [earnestly] mindful of His covenant and forever it is imprinted on His heart, the word which He commanded and established to a thousand generations **(Psalm 105:8)**

Nothing that you could ever gain in this world will compare to the LOVE that awakens you and the LOVE that keeps you throughout the day.

Whom have I in heaven but You? And I have no delight or desire on earth besides You **(Psalm 73:25)**

How we define our storm is a direct reflection of how we define our God. If God says: In the storm, I AM WITH YOU, and the floods WIL NOT OVERTAKE YOU…then TRUST THAT!!! We can continue to quote His Word, or we can actually be partakers of His promises.

_____

_____

_____

_____

_____

_____

_____

_____

_____

_____

_____

_____

_____

_____

_____

_____

_____

_____

_____

_____

_____

_____

_____

Salvation belongs to the Lord; May Your blessing be upon Your people **(Psalm 3:8)**

Only intimate fellowship with God's LOVE beckons us and causes us to surrender. We understand nothing is done in our own strength and our need for Him is as the air we breathe.

_____

_____

_____

_____

_____

_____

_____

_____

_____

_____

_____

_____

_____

_____

_____

_____

_____

_____

_____

_____

_____

_____

Cast your burden on the Lord, releasing the weight of it, and He will sustain you; He will never allow the righteous, birth by faith in Jesus Christ, to be moved (made to slip, fall, or fail **(Psalm 55:22)**

Religion without love often teaches men how to meet a moral standard and possess riches, power, and the praise of men, yet it leaves us empty; but only in a relationship with God are we COMPLETE, WHOLE, & LACK NOTHING!

_____

_____

_____

_____

_____

_____

_____

_____

_____

_____

_____

_____

_____

_____

_____

_____

_____

_____

_____

_____

_____

_____

He refreshes and restores my life and all in my life; He leads me in the paths of righteousness (uprightness and right standing with Him, and not for my earning it, but) for His name's sake **(Psalm 23:3)**

As long as we seek an external experience with God, a counterfeit can be produced. We will have counterfeit productions of blessings, but lack a change of heart.

_____

_____

_____

_____

_____

_____

_____

_____

_____

_____

_____

_____

_____

_____

_____

_____

_____

_____

The Lord is my Rock, my Fortress, and my Deliverer; my God, my keen and firm Strength in Whom I will trust and take refuge, my Shield, and the Horn of my salvation, my High Tower **(Psalm 18:2)**

It is NOT all the things we do that overwhelms us, it's the ONE thing we don't: GET ALONE WITH GOD. Time spent with the Father is priceless, there's absolutely nothing like His presence!

_____

_____

_____

_____

_____

_____

_____

_____

_____

_____

_____

_____

_____

_____

_____

_____

_____

_____

_____

Let, I pray You, Your merciful kindness and steadfast love be for my comfort, according to Your promise to Your servant **(Psalm 119:76)**.

The grace of God has the ability to utterly and wholly permeate our lives. Just know that failure and weakness are absolutely irrelevant in the face of such all-pervading grace.

_____

_____

_____

_____

_____

_____

_____

_____

_____

_____

_____

_____

_____

_____

_____

_____

_____

_____

_____

_____

Yes, the Lord will provide what is good, and our land will yield its increase **(Psalm 85:15)**

The dismantling of our human efforts and efforts of others is the ONE thing that will bring us face to face with God. Farther today may we recognize you are our ONLY option and means to WHOLENESS. May we end our panting after dry places and receive Your living water.

Great peace have they who love Your Word; nothing shall offend them or make them stumble **(Psalm 119:165)**

Always remember the Peace and Rest that comes from abiding in God's presence is the true substance of life....all this other stuff we do are momentary fixes. He alone fills all in all!

_____

_____

_____

_____

_____

_____

_____

_____

_____

_____

_____

_____

_____

_____

_____

_____

_____

_____

Arouse Yourself, awake to the justice due me, even to my cause, my God and my Lord **(Psalm 35:23)**

Stop fighting a fight that's already WON!!!!! So thankful to Christ, who is and will always be the Mighty Lion of Judah and our Conquering King. Nothing like His Peace in the midst of confusion.

_____

_____

_____

_____

_____

_____

_____

_____

_____

_____

_____

_____

_____

_____

_____

_____

_____

_____

_____

_____

Lord, how many and varied are Your works! In wisdom have You made them all; the earth is full of Your riches and Your creatures **(Psalm 104:24)**

We rarely have a problem identifying with God as our powerful provider, being able to help us overcome our circumstances. Yes, he is a God of power, a God of deliverance, a God of victory, but we forget that he is also a God of love, a God of peace, a God of integrity, and a patient God.

_____

_____

_____

_____

_____

_____

_____

_____

_____

_____

_____

_____

_____

_____

_____

_____

_____

_____

_____

_____

_____

He heals the brokenhearted and binds up their wounds curing their pains and their sorrows **(Psalm 147:3)**

Father today we recognize that you not only desire to deliver us but you desire our WHOLENESS and a complete work to be done within us. May we SEEK not only to be delivered, but to also walk worthy of being called Abba's child!

_____

_____

_____

_____

_____

_____

_____

_____

_____

_____

_____

_____

_____

_____

_____

_____

_____

_____

_____

_____

_____

_____

The Lord bless you and keep you. The Lord make His face to shine upon you and be gracious to you. The Lord lift up His countenance upon you and give you peace. **(Num 6:24-26)**

Recognize being at war with others take you completely out of the peace of God.

_____

_____

_____

_____

_____

_____

_____

_____

_____

_____

_____

_____

_____

_____

_____

_____

_____

_____

_____

_____

_____

_____

How precious is Your steadfast love, oh God! We take refuge in the shadow of your wings. **(Psalm 36:7)**

May we enter and remain in divine REST. Cease from your works and completely surrender to magnificent and capable power of the Holy Spirit to accomplish God's will through you and for you.

_____

_____

_____

_____

_____

_____

_____

_____

_____

_____

_____

_____

_____

_____

_____

_____

_____

_____

_____

But let those who take refuge in God rejoice; for You have spread Your protection over them. For you bless and cover the righteous with favor as a shield. **(Psalms 5:11-12)**

Sorrow is just that, an emotion resulting from our interpretation of our current position; it has nothing to do with the Power of God to be ALL we need Him to be in our midst.

_____

_____

_____

_____

_____

_____

_____

_____

_____

_____

_____

_____

_____

_____

_____

_____

_____

_____

_____

_____

_____

This I will say about my Father, He is my refuge and my fortress, my God, in whom I trust **(Psalm 91:2)**.

Father, we declare a changing of the guards today. We will Guard our mind with Your truth. May we let only Your Word be at the door post of our hearts, minds, and lips, and embrace a life of trust and freedom.

_____

_____

_____

_____

_____

_____

_____

_____

_____

_____

_____

_____

_____

_____

_____

_____

_____

_____

_____

_____

_____

_____

_____

This is my comfort and consolation in my affliction: that Your word has revived me and given me life **(Psalm 119:50)**.

Father today we stand with the Sword of the Spirit, the great weapon of warfare, penetrating every stronghold, worldly mindset, and unprofitable word spoken over our lives. We surrender to Your divine truth about our life and stand victorious over ALL hindering circumstances.

_____

_____

_____

_____

_____

_____

_____

_____

_____

_____

_____

_____

_____

_____

_____

_____

_____

_____

_____

Show me your ways Oh Lord; teach me your paths. Lead me in your truth and teach me, for you are the God of my salvation; on you I will wait all the day. **(Psalm 25:4-5)**.

Today we silence our frustrations by declaring Your All Powerful Logos. Now may the darkness of our understanding be enlightened as walk through this day victorious, being kept by the power of unfailing Your Love.

_____

_____

_____

_____

_____

_____

_____

_____

_____

_____

_____

_____

_____

_____

_____

_____

_____

_____

You have multiplied, O LORD my God, your wondrous deeds and your thoughts toward us; none can compare with you! I will proclaim and tell of them, yet they are more than can be told. **(Psalm 40:5)**.

Thank you for your eternal love today Father. It is the only garrison of our soul. May we meditate on Your awesome love that has been poured out without measure. Your love equals our peace every time, so may we gaze intently upon it today.

_____

_____

_____

_____

_____

_____

_____

_____

_____

_____

_____

_____

_____

_____

_____

_____

_____

_____

_____

Whom have I in Heaven but there? And there is nothing upon earth that I desire besides thee. My flesh and my heart may fail, but God is the strength of my heart and my portion forever. **(Psalm 73:25-26)**

Today we REST & RECEIVE! Father we thank you that wisdom and direction is provided by the unction of your Holy Spirit on today. Let us receive your given rest in all things. Teach us to receive Holy Spirit, not based on our works, but based on the love and finished work of Christ.

_____

_____

_____

_____

_____

_____

_____

_____

_____

_____

_____

_____

_____

_____

_____

_____

_____

_____

_____

_____

Now may the God of peace, who through the blood of the eternal covenant brought back from the dead our Lord Jesus, that great Shepherd of the sheep, equip you with everything good for doing his will, and may he work in us what is pleasing to him, through Jesus Christ, to whom be glory for ever and ever. Amen. **(Hebrews 13:20-21)**

We boldly confess our desires, whether wrong or right, selfish or godly, we still boldly confess them, trusting that you and only you will purify our hearts and transform our wills by the power of your Holy Spirit. We wait for you, we long and thirst for a continual abiding.

_____

_____

_____

_____

_____

_____

_____

_____

_____

_____

_____

_____

_____

_____

_____

_____

_____

_____

_____

_____

_____

You will keep him in perfect peace whose mind is stayed on You because he trusts You. Trust in The Lord forever, for The Lord God is an everlasting Rock. Oh Lord, You will ordain peace for us, for it is You that has established our works. **(Isaiah 26:3-4; 12)**.

God will empower you to love Him by revealing His great love for you day after day! Ask Him for revelation.

_____

_____

_____

_____

_____

_____

_____

_____

_____

_____

_____

_____

_____

_____

_____

_____

_____

_____

_____

_____

_____

The weapon that has been formed against you will NEVER prosper, but know without a doubt God's plans to prosper you will **(Isa. 54:17; Jer. 29:11)**.

Sometimes where God has you and even where He is sending you is not where you will end up. Be of GOOD CHEER and TRUST the process. It's not over!

_____

_____

_____

_____

_____

_____

_____

_____

_____

_____

_____

_____

_____

_____

_____

_____

_____

_____

_____

_____

_____

_____

_____

_____

_____

My soul, wait thou only upon God. **(Ps. 62:5)**

Father, we no longer deny You access to our heart to deal with those things hidden from public sight. You have knocked and waited patiently at the door of our heart to bring healing and freedom. Today, we open our heart fully to You, ACCESS GRANTED!

_____

_____

_____

_____

_____

_____

_____

_____

_____

_____

_____

_____

_____

_____

_____

_____

_____

_____

_____

_____

_____

_____

_____

You make known to me the path of life; in Your presence there is fullness of joy; at Your right hand are pleasures forevermore **(Psalm 16:11)**.

Father may we recognize that You alone are the "Healing" for what has wounded us. You don't just provide healing but you make us WHOLE. May we turn our hearts and faces towards You and find the forgiveness we need to offer those who have wounded us.

_____

_____

_____

_____

_____

_____

_____

_____

_____

_____

_____

_____

_____

_____

_____

_____

_____

_____

_____

_____

_____

_____

If we are faithless, He remains faithful; for He can not deny Himself **(2 Tim 2:13)**.

Father, today we receive the breath of Your Spirit that make us a living witness of Your Love. For You have quickened and made alive in us Your Divine Will. Today we walk with a living HOPE knowing it's Your grace and mercy that is leading, guiding, and watching over us to perform Your good in our life.

The eternal God is your refuge and dwelling place, and underneath are the everlasting arms; He drove the enemy before you and thrust them out, saying, Destroy **(Deuteronomy 33:27)**.

Father, let Your precious Holy Spirt do ALL for us on today. Where we are weak, may You strengthen us and where we lack wisdom, may You shine Your heavenly light and give us truth that dispels all lies. Be with us on this blessed and prosperous day!

_____

_____

_____

_____

_____

_____

_____

_____

_____

_____

_____

_____

_____

_____

_____

_____

_____

_____

_____

My God, my Rock, in Him will I take refuge; my Shield and the Horn of my salvation; my Stronghold and my Refuge, my Savior--You save me from violence **(2 Samuel 22:3)**.

God works miracles with marred clay! There is nothing like the Potter's hands molding your life.

_____

_____

_____

_____

_____

_____

_____

_____

_____

_____

_____

_____

_____

_____

_____

_____

_____

_____

_____

But let all those who take refuge and put their trust in You rejoice; let them ever sing and shout for joy, because You make a covering over them and defend them; let those also who love Your name be joyful in You and be in high spirits **(Psalm 5:11)**.

Our greatest discouragement, distress, and discontentment results from a lack of trust in the one who ordains life by the counsel of His will. Let go and TRUST.

_____

_____

_____

_____

_____

_____

_____

_____

_____

_____

_____

_____

_____

_____

_____

_____

_____

BE MERCIFUL and gracious to me, O God, be merciful and gracious to me, for my soul takes refuge and finds shelter and confidence in You; yes, in the shadow of Your wings will I take refuge and be confident until calamities and destructive storms are passed **(Psalm 57:1)**.

That moment when you realize God's hand has guided your entire life and you just have to say thank you for it all. Never ask WHY, say thank you and know whatever it is, IT is working for your good!

_____

_____

_____

_____

_____

_____

_____

_____

_____

_____

_____

_____

_____

_____

_____

_____

_____

_____

_____

_____

_____

This is my comfort and consolation in my affliction: that Your word has revived me and given me life **(Psalm 119:50)**.

I can never repay You Lord for what you've done for me; how you loosed my shackles and set me free; how you made a way out no way and turned my darkness into day; You've been my joy in the time of sorrow, my hope for tomorrow; peace in the times of storm and my strength when I'm weak and worn. ~Eddie James

_____

_____

_____

_____

_____

_____

_____

_____

_____

_____

_____

_____

_____

_____

_____

_____

_____

For the Lord will comfort Zion; He will comfort all her waste places. And He will make her wilderness like Eden, and her desert like the garden of the Lord. Joy and gladness will be found in her, thanksgiving and the voice of song or instrument of praise **(Isaiah 51:3)**.

Today Father we open our hearts to receive what You have already given and have longed for us to walk boldly in.

Blessed be the God and Father of our Lord Jesus Christ, the Father of sympathy and the God of every comfort. Who comforts us in every trouble, so that we may also be able to comfort those who are in any kind of trouble or distress, with the comfort with which we ourselves are comforted by God **(2 Corinthians 1:3-4)**.

Today may we perceive what is divinely designed for the perfection of Your will in our lives. May true joy flood and satisfy our soul and be our ever abiding strength.

_____

_____

_____

_____

_____

_____

_____

_____

_____

_____

_____

_____

_____

_____

_____

_____

_____

_____

_____

So we take comfort and are encouraged and confidently and boldly say, The Lord is my Helper; I will not be seized with alarm [I will not fear or dread or be terrified]. What can man do to me (Hebrews 13:6). ✓

There is something about thanking and praising the Father when there is no sign of deliverance. He often told His children to praise in the heat of the battle. Their praise was indicative of their trust in Him, and it also brought confusion to the destructive plans of their enemies. Know that your God is a Mighty Fortress and a Conquering King for you. May your faith produce abounding joy and total victory (nothing missing and nothing broken) today and forevermore.

And there I will sustain and provide for you, so that you and your household and all that are yours may not come to poverty and want, for there are yet five [more] years of [the scarcity, hunger, and starvation of] famine **(Genesis 45:15)**

The safest place is in the steadfast arms of God's love that is our constant shelter whether we recognize or accept it as being so. Father let Your mercy always prevail.

_____

_____

_____

_____

_____

_____

_____

_____

_____

_____

_____

_____

_____

_____

_____

_____

_____

_____

_____

_____

_____

Let those who favor my righteous cause and have pleasure in my uprightness shout for joy and be glad and say continually, Let the Lord be magnified, Who takes pleasure in the (provision) and prosperity of His servant **(Psalm 35:27).**

In and of ourselves we can do nothing. If a man think he is something, he soon finds he is nothing without the Power of God's Spirit. Pride leads to failure, but true humility creates peace and a prosperous life.

_____

_____

_____

_____

_____

_____

_____

_____

_____

_____

_____

_____

_____

_____

_____

_____

_____

_____

_____

_____

_____

You visit the earth and saturate it with water; You greatly enrich it; the river of God is full of water; You provide them with grain when You have so prepared the earth **(Psalm 65:9)**.

Many things are possible for the person who has HOPE. Even more things are possible for the person who has FAITH. Still more is possible for the person who walks in LOVE. But everything is possible for the person who practices all three. ~Brother Lawrence, The Practice of the Presence of God

And God Who provides seed for the sower and bread for eating will also provide and multiply your resources for sowing and increase the fruits of your righteousness which manifests itself in active goodness, kindness, and charity **(2 Corinthians 9:10)**.

There are days when the Father has to MAKE you lie down in green pastures. Nothing like the GOOD Shepherd!!!!!

_____

_____

_____

_____

_____

_____

_____

_____

_____

_____

_____

_____

_____

_____

_____

_____

_____

_____

_____

_____

For the LORD giveth wisdom: out of his mouth cometh knowledge and understanding **(Proverbs 2:6).**

How many times has the "seed" of a "life changing" word been sown in your heart but seemed to slowly produce or yield its fruit? Many times we leave that seed untended and the process of manifestation is slow and painful. Always surrender the ground of your heart to God's word, fully. Don't allow the enemy, circumstances, or wrong thinking to hinder your divine purpose any longer.

And wisdom and knowledge shall be the stability of thy times, and strength of salvation: the fear of the LORD is his treasure **(Isaiah 33:6)**

There are times when it seems God is silent to our cries, but not one sound ever goes unheard. Sometimes the Father is pruning our hearts that we will go from just bearing fruit to bearing much fruit. Count it ALL joy!

_____

_____

_____

_____

_____

_____

_____

_____

_____

_____

_____

_____

_____

_____

_____

_____

_____

_____

_____

_____

_____

But unto them which are called, both Jews and Greeks, Christ the power of God, and the wisdom of God **(1 Corinthians 1:24)**

WHOLENESS produces humility. Greatness is never determined by how high you can go, but greatness is determined in how low you a willing to go to be an instrument in the Father's hand.

_____

_____

_____

_____

_____

_____

_____

_____

_____

_____

_____

_____

_____

_____

_____

_____

_____

_____

_____

_____

_____

_____

You are a hiding place for me; You, Lord, preserve me from trouble, You surround me with songs and shouts of deliverance **(Psalm 32:7)**

Always consider your motives. That practice will avert many destructive decisions made and outcomes experienced.

Because he has set his love upon Me, therefore will I deliver him; I will set him on high, because he knows and understands My name [has a personal knowledge of My mercy, love, and kindness--trusts and relies on Me, knowing I will never forsake him, no, never] **(Psalm 91:14)**

When being used to bless the lives of others, I have found that we are small creatures in the hands of an extraordinary and magnificent God. His power far exceed our ability. May we yield even more to the grace that anoints our service.

_____

_____

_____

_____

_____

_____

_____

_____

_____

_____

_____

_____

_____

_____

_____

_____

_____

_____

_____

_____

_____

_____

_____

Deliver and Save my life, O Lord, for Your name's sake; in Your righteousness, bring my life out of trouble and free me from distress **(Psalm 143:11)**

You can't manage another person's thoughts about you. When you try, you fall prey to leaving the post of your own thoughts/mind unguarded. Beware of distractions and "distractors" from God's divine plan and purpose!

_____

_____

_____

_____

_____

_____

_____

_____

_____

_____

_____

_____

_____

_____

_____

_____

_____

_____

_____

_____

The Lord your God is in the midst of you, a Mighty One, a Savior [Who saves]! He will rejoice over you with joy; He will rest [in silent satisfaction] and in His love He will be silent and make no mention [of past sins, or even recall them]; He will exult over you with singing **(Zephaniah 3:17)**

Abba, I stand in awe of You! From the foundations of the earth You have declared Your love and established Your dominion. Your hand print will forever be pressed upon my heart and life.

_____

_____

_____

_____

_____

_____

_____

_____

_____

_____

_____

_____

_____

_____

_____

_____

_____

_____

_____

ANSWER ME when I call, O God of my righteousness (uprightness, justice, and right standing with You)! You have freed me when I was hemmed in and enlarged me when I was in distress; have mercy upon me and hear my prayer **(Psalm 4:1)**

We often seek things we are not naturally or spiritually prepared for. Allow God to prepare and position you to be blessed and to be a blessing.

_____

_____

_____

_____

_____

_____

_____

_____

_____

_____

_____

_____

_____

_____

_____

_____

_____

_____

_____

_____

_____

Righteousness and justice are the foundation of Your throne; mercy and loving-kindness and truth go before Your face **(Psalm 89:14)**

Father we invite Your providential hand to guide our thoughts, actions, and ultimately our life. May we trust in Your divine process as You show us how to respond to the delays, distractions, and disappointments.

_____

_____

_____

_____

_____

_____

_____

_____

_____

_____

_____

_____

_____

_____

_____

_____

_____

_____

For justice will return to the [uncompromisingly] righteous, and all the upright in heart will follow it **(Psalm 94:15)**

When our vision is not congruent with God's purpose it creates a sense of stagnation and frustration. Instead of forcing your plans into existence, be still and know that God is positioning you for His glory and your greatest good. Be patient, it's His love that is constraining you from accepting less than His best.

_____

_____

_____

_____

_____

_____

_____

_____

_____

_____

_____

_____

_____

_____

_____

_____

_____

_____

_____

I know and rest in confidence upon it that the Lord will maintain the cause of the afflicted, and will secure justice for the poor and needy (of His believing children) **(Psalm 140:12).**

Be careful of the thoughts you entertain, they may cause your heart to filled with regret and disappointment. Be thankful and allow your gratitude to harness your own unique greatness given to you by the Father.

_____

_____

_____

_____

_____

_____

_____

_____

_____

_____

_____

_____

_____

_____

_____

_____

_____

_____

_____

_____

_____

But He was wounded for our transgressions, He was bruised for our guilt and iniquities; the chastisement [needful to obtain] peace and well-being for us was upon Him, and with the stripes [that wounded] Him we are healed and made whole **(Isaiah 53:5)**

Find the miracle, blessing, joy, etc. in your own life and never covet another's life. God has richly blessed us all.

_____

_____

_____

_____

_____

_____

_____

_____

_____

_____

_____

_____

_____

_____

_____

_____

_____

_____

_____

_____

Heal me, O Lord, and I shall be healed; save me, and I shall be saved, for You are my praise **(Jeremiah 17:14)**

Father there is no fulfillment outside of You. You are my portion, the ONLY internal and eternal satisfaction. Not even my good works answer the longing in my soul. For it is Your presence alone that delivers and ravishes my soul with JOY. You are my TRUE PLEASURE!

_____

_____

_____

_____

_____

_____

_____

_____

_____

_____

_____

_____

_____

_____

_____

_____

_____

And the Lord shall guide you continually and satisfy you in drought and in dry places and make strong your bones. And you shall be like a watered garden and like a spring of water whose waters fail not **(Isaiah 58:11)**

It's not over until God says its over. SO, count it ALL JOY. He will make ALL things NEW.

_____

_____

_____

_____

_____

_____

_____

_____

_____

_____

_____

_____

_____

_____

_____

_____

_____

_____

_____

In peace I will both lie down and sleep, for You, Lord, alone make me dwell in safety and confident trust **(Psalm 4:8)**

Neglect of any kind can often strip a person of self-worth making it difficult for them to experience inner peace or true contentment. Father we pray for Your restorative power today, make new the broken places of our hearts, and may we know, see, and receive Your divine purpose and promises for our life.

_____

_____

_____

_____

_____

_____

_____

_____

_____

_____

_____

_____

_____

_____

_____

_____

_____

_____

But the meek [in the end] shall inherit the earth and shall delight themselves in the abundance of peace **(Psalm 37:11)**

Your deliverance is not a matter of the Father's ability to deliver you, but your ability to receive. Connect consciously as often as you can to God's Word of faith and promise until you see what the He has already envisioned for your life.

_____

_____

_____

_____

_____

_____

_____

_____

_____

_____

_____

_____

_____

_____

_____

_____

_____

_____

_____

_____

_____

May peace be within your walls and prosperity within your palaces **(Psalm 122:7)**

Father may you open our eyes to see the enormity of Your grace and mercy in our own life. We have plenty to praise You for.

_____

_____

_____

_____

_____

_____

_____

_____

_____

_____

_____

_____

_____

_____

_____

_____

_____

_____

_____

_____

And the peace of God, which passeth all understanding, shall keep your hearts and minds through Christ Jesus **(Philippians 4:7)**

Not just for one moment, but forever You will satisfy the thirsty soul. You were poured out as a drink offering to fill the heart that welcomes You.

_____

_____

_____

_____

_____

_____

_____

_____

_____

_____

_____

_____

_____

_____

_____

_____

_____

_____

_____

_____

_____

_____

_____

Now may the Lord of peace Himself grant you His peace (the peace of His kingdom) at all times and in all ways [under all circumstances and conditions, whatever comes]. The Lord [be] with you all **(2 Thessalonians 3:16)**

Sometimes you have to sow into someone else field to reap your harvest. Stop looking to see what you can get, rather be a blessing and give.

_____

_____

_____

_____

_____

_____

_____

_____

_____

_____

_____

_____

_____

_____

_____

_____

_____

_____

_____

_____

_____

_____

_____

You are a hiding place for me; You, Lord, preserve me from trouble, You surround me with songs and shouts of deliverance **(Psalm 32:7)**

When a word is needed, God will give it. When direction is needed, God will give it. When clarity/vision is needed, God will give it. Be still and know that He is God and has made all provision for you and when it is needed, HE will give it.

_____

_____

_____

_____

_____

_____

_____

_____

_____

_____

_____

_____

_____

_____

_____

_____

_____

_____

_____

_____

_____

_____

But thanks be to God, Who gives us the victory [making us conquerors] through our Lord Jesus Christ **(1 Corinthians 15:57)**

Don't pay a high price for things of no value, when the Spirit is offering TRUE LIFE freely.

_____

_____

_____

_____

_____

_____

_____

_____

_____

_____

_____

_____

_____

_____

_____

_____

_____

_____

_____

_____

_____

For whatever is born of God is victorious over the world; and this is the victory that conquers the world, even our faith **(1 John 5:4)**

In Your presence God, my fear has no place, my doubt has no place, my worry has no place, my pride has no place. May I NEVER forget that your LOVE has dismantled the power of my enemy.

_____

_____

_____

_____

_____

_____

_____

_____

_____

_____

_____

_____

_____

_____

_____

_____

_____

_____

_____

_____

_____

_____

Restore to me the joy of Your salvation and uphold me with a willing spirit **(Psalm 51:12)**

Cut through these chains that tie me down to so many lesser things, until all my dreams fall to the ground and this one remains: my magnificent obsession. ~Steven Curtis Chapman

Turn us to Yourself, O Lord, and we shall be turned and restored! Renew our days as of old **(Lamentations 5:21)**

Father with Your love and truth You comfort and secure my soul. May I abide in Your presence and make manifest Your glory today. For it is Your strength that gird up my weakness and make living for You possible. Keep me in the center of Your will.

_____

_____

_____

_____

_____

_____

_____

_____

_____

_____

_____

_____

_____

_____

_____

_____

_____

_____

_____

_____

_____

And your ancient ruins shall be rebuilt; you shall raise up the foundations of many generations; and you shall be called Repairer of the Breach, Restorer of Streets to Dwell In **(Isaiah 58:12)**

Our futile attempt to please others is a blatant disregard for the Father's perfect love and full acceptance of who we truly are. His love goes beyond our works or lack thereof.

_____

_____

_____

_____

_____

_____

_____

_____

_____

_____

_____

_____

_____

_____

_____

_____

_____

_____

_____

Return to the stronghold [of security and prosperity], you prisoners of hope; even today do I declare that I will restore double your former prosperity to you **(Zechariah 9:12)**

I have done nothing for Him, but He has done all for me. He has relentlessly pursued our hearts. What manner of love is this bestowed upon us by the Father. May we lay down all our loves for the greatest of them all.

_____

_____

_____

_____

_____

_____

_____

_____

_____

_____

_____

_____

_____

_____

_____

_____

_____

_____

_____

You will show me the path of life; in Your presence is fullness of joy, at Your right hand there are pleasures forevermore **(Psalms 16:11)**

God know just how much pressure to apply to bring forth BIRTH and BREAKTHROUGH in your life. Transform us oh God!

_____

_____

_____

_____

_____

_____

_____

_____

_____

_____

_____

_____

_____

_____

_____

_____

_____

_____

My whole being shall be satisfied as with marrow and fatness; and my mouth shall praise You with joyful lips, only when I remember you upon my bed and mediate on You in the night watches. **(Psalm 63:4-5)**

Our greatest weapon "sometimes" is silence. Sometimes we talk too much. Be quick to listen, slow to speak (James 1:19)

May the God of your hope so fill you with all joy and peace in believing [through the experience of your faith] that by the power of the Holy Spirit you may abound and be overflowing (bubbling over) with hope **(Romans 15:13)**

Sometimes God authors peace in strange ways, like severing relationships we are vested in more than we are vested in Him. Father, help our minds to be stayed on YOU, the only source of true peace.

_____

_____

_____

_____

_____

_____

_____

_____

_____

_____

_____

_____

_____

_____

_____

_____

_____

He asked life of You, and You gave it to him--long life forever and evermore **(Psalm 21:4)**

Cease the excessive mind chatter and quiet your spirit. I, The Lord desire to order your steps, to lead you into the way of peace and WHOLENESS.

He refreshes and restores my life (my self); He leads me in the paths of righteousness [uprightness and right standing with Him--not for my earning it, but] for His name's sake **(Psalm 23:3)**

The chaotic stream of thinking prevents you from hearing me. I am speaking; be still and listen, then will your way be made clear and direction be given.

_____

_____

_____

_____

_____

_____

_____

_____

_____

_____

_____

_____

_____

_____

_____

_____

_____

_____

THE LORD is my Light and my Salvation--whom shall I fear or dread? The Lord is the Refuge and Stronghold of my life--of whom shall I be afraid **(Psalm 27:1)**

Father let all un-surrendered places give way. Let the walls that keep Your love from pouring in and pouring out, fall to the ground. May we come out of denial this day and walk in the light of Your Truth and Freedom.

_____

_____

_____

_____

_____

_____

_____

_____

_____

_____

_____

_____

_____

_____

_____

_____

_____

_____

_____

_____

_____

My life makes its boast in the Lord; let the humble and afflicted hear and be glad **(Psalm 34:12)**

Father, You are my chief pursuit, the magnificent obsession of my heart. I'm lost without You, let Your love be a divine compass to the sweet surrender of my soul. I leave all behind and I'm running to You, my answer.

_____

_____

_____

_____

_____

_____

_____

_____

_____

_____

_____

_____

_____

_____

_____

_____

_____

_____

_____

_____

_____

I lay down and slept; I wakened again, for the Lord sustains me **(Psalm 3:5)**

Invade this earthly temple; sanctify it for Your Glory. Not our will Father; we lay it down, oh God. Holy fire purge this heart that is laid before You. Only the broken and contrite You will not despise. Forever oh King Your bride will praise You.

_____

_____

_____

_____

_____

_____

_____

_____

_____

_____

_____

_____

_____

_____

_____

_____

_____

Cast your burden on the Lord [releasing the weight of it] and He will sustain you; He will never allow the [consistently] righteous to be moved (made to slip, fall, or fail) **(Psalm 55:22)**

Father Your Spirit has drawn us into a loving relationship. It wasn't the chastisement of Your rod used to draw us, but it was a gift, wrapped in humility. May we be imitators of Christ as dear children.

The Lord is your keeper; the Lord is your shade on your right hand [the side not carrying a shield] **(Psalm 121:5)**

Insecurity is filled with vain philosophies and boastings that are void of the Holy Spirit. Live, Move, and have your Being in identity that is given from your Heavenly Father.

_____

_____

_____

_____

_____

_____

_____

_____

_____

_____

_____

_____

_____

_____

_____

_____

_____

_____

_____

_____

_____

_____

_____

_____

I, the Lord, am its Keeper; I water it every moment; lest anyone harm it, I guard and keep it night and day **(Isaiah 27:3)**

Father whom in heaven do we have besides You, and whom on earth do We desire but You? Try as we might to seek outside of You, it only leads to desolation, disappointment, and destruction. Your love knows NO distance; approach our hearts, for today we welcome You in.

_____

_____

_____

_____

_____

_____

_____

_____

_____

_____

_____

_____

_____

_____

_____

_____

_____

_____

_____

_____

_____

_____

I will cry to God Most High, Who performs on my behalf and rewards me [Who brings to pass His purposes for me and surely completes them] **(Psalm 57:2)**

Allow the Holy Spirit rebuild, restore, revive, and renew all broken areas of your life. Allow Him to occupy those hurt places. Occupy Holy Spirit our temples. Rebuild the broken down walls of our hearts. Restore and make us permeable for Your Spirit only.

_____

_____

_____

_____

_____

_____

_____

_____

_____

_____

_____

_____

_____

_____

_____

_____

_____

_____

_____

_____

_____

For this is My Father's will and His purpose, that everyone who sees the Son and believes in and cleaves to and trusts in and relies on Him should have eternal life, and I will raise him up [from the dead] at the last day **(John 6:40)**

Father thank you for Your everlasting covenant You made with Us. Our faith is anchored in Your faithfulness; that if You promised, You will bring it to pass.

_____

_____

_____

_____

_____

_____

_____

_____

_____

_____

_____

_____

_____

_____

_____

_____

_____

_____

_____

_____

_____

For we are God's [own] handiwork (His workmanship) recreated in Christ Jesus, [born anew] that we may do those good works which God predestined (planned beforehand) for us [taking paths which He prepared ahead of time], that we should walk in them [living the good life which He prearranged and made ready for us to live] **(Ephesians 2:10)**

Teach us Holy Spirit to wait patiently upon The Lord that our strength may be renewed for our upcoming journey.

_____

_____

_____

_____

_____

_____

_____

_____

_____

_____

_____

_____

_____

_____

_____

_____

_____

_____

_____

And the world passes away and disappears, and with it the forbidden cravings (the passionate desires, the lust) of it; but he who does the will of God and carries out His purposes in his life abides (remains) forever **(1 John 2:17)**

Father above all else may we have a deep, full, abiding, and overwhelming experience of Your love on today. May it overflow and be shared with those around me.

_____

_____

_____

_____

_____

_____

_____

_____

_____

_____

_____

_____

_____

_____

_____

_____

_____

_____

_____

With long life will I satisfy him and show him My salvation **(Psalm 91:16)**

Father transform us into the image of Your dear Son. Cover and empower us with the grace of Your Holy Spirit to bring glory to Your name. We are incapable of bearing fruit without the indwelling of Your Holy Spirit.

_____

_____

_____

_____

_____

_____

_____

_____

_____

_____

_____

_____

_____

_____

_____

_____

_____

_____

_____

_____

_____

Behold, God is my salvation; I will trust and not be afraid: for the Lord JEHOVAH is my strength and my song; yes He has become my salvation. Therefore, with joy shall we draw from the wells of salvation **(Isaiah 12:2-3)**

Who are we without the light and love that reveals grace within every breath we take and every step we make. Take today to meditate on grace that guides your life.

_____

_____

_____

_____

_____

_____

_____

_____

_____

_____

_____

_____

_____

_____

_____

_____

_____

_____

_____

_____

As for me, I will continue beholding Your face in righteousness (rightness, justice, and right standing with You); I shall be fully satisfied, when I awake [to find myself] beholding Your form [and having sweet communion with You] **(Psalm 17:15)**

Father let today be the day we refuse to apologize for who You are to us, in us, and through us because someone doesn't understand or is intimidated by Your glory. Let us shine forth Your love and Your glory in the unique ways You have made us.

_____

_____

_____

_____

_____

_____

_____

_____

_____

_____

_____

_____

_____

_____

_____

_____

_____

_____

_____

_____

In Your name they rejoice all the day, and in Your righteousness they are exalted **(Psalm 89:16)**

Letting go is a choice. It is a choice many are not willing to make because they believe to let go is to lose what you hoped for.

_____

_____

_____

_____

_____

_____

_____

_____

_____

_____

_____

_____

_____

_____

_____

_____

_____

_____

_____

_____

_____

For I know that my redeemer liveth, and that he shall stand at the latter day upon the earth **(Job 19:25)**

There is a point where you have to surrender to this truth: there is but ONE SOURCE of PEACE, one source of JOY, one source of WHOLENESS; and that source lives inside of you

_____

_____

_____

_____

_____

_____

_____

_____

_____

_____

_____

_____

_____

_____

_____

_____

_____

_____

_____

Thus saith the LORD, thy redeemer, and he that formed thee from the womb, I am the LORD that makes all things; that stretches forth the heavens alone; that spreads abroad the earth by myself **(Isaiah 44:24)**

God surpasses our dreams when we reach pass our personal plans and agenda to grab the hand of Christ and walk the path he chose for us. He is obligated to keep us dissatisfied until we come to him and his plan for complete satisfaction. ~Beth Moore

_____

_____

_____

_____

_____

_____

_____

_____

_____

_____

_____

_____

_____

_____

_____

_____

_____

_____

_____

_____

Thus says the Lord, the King of Israel and his Redeemer, the Lord of hosts: I am the First and I am the Last; besides Me there is no God **(Isaiah 44:6)**

Faith is the power to stand up to the madness and chaos of the physical world while holding the position that nothing external has ay authority over what heaven has in mind for you. ~Caroline Myss

_____

_____

_____

_____

_____

_____

_____

_____

_____

_____

_____

_____

_____

_____

_____

_____

_____

_____

_____

_____

_____

_____

_____

And I will establish My covenant with you, and you shall know (understand and realize) that I am the Lord **(Ezekiel 16:62)**

Sometimes we are kept in situations until the full embodiment of Christ takes place within us. So instead of looking to the Father to let you out of it, ask Him to TRANSFORM you in it...Only then can you transition through it.

_____

_____

_____

_____

_____

_____

_____

_____

_____

_____

_____

_____

_____

_____

_____

_____

_____

_____

_____

Be mindful of His covenant forever, the promise which He commanded and established to a thousand generations **(1 Chronicles 16;15)**

In silence the Father whispers: I'm not withholding the answers to your prayers; it's just you are asking for the wrong things; you are asking for things that are momentary and will perish. Be still and discern my perfect will, that I have given to you freely.

_____

_____

_____

_____

_____

_____

_____

_____

_____

_____

_____

_____

_____

_____

_____

_____

_____

_____

_____

Let, I pray You, Your merciful kindness and steadfast love be for my comfort, according to Your promise to Your servant **(Psalm 119:65)**

Ask me for what your heart truly desires and longs for, for those things will be given instantly. Is it complete rest and peace; it's yours. Is it provision; already yours. Is it joy unspeakable; it's yours. Is it abounding grace; it's yours. Is it an everlasting love; it's certainly yours.

_____

_____

_____

_____

_____

_____

_____

_____

_____

_____

_____

_____

_____

_____

_____

_____

_____

_____

_____

_____

_____

Fully satisfied and assured that God was able and mighty to keep His word and to do what He had promised **(Romans 4:21)**

No one who knows who God made them to be desires to be anyone else.
~Bill Johnson

_____

_____

_____

_____

_____

_____

_____

_____

_____

_____

_____

_____

_____

_____

_____

_____

_____

_____

_____

_____

_____

_____

_____

_____

Whom have I in heaven but You? And I have no delight or desire on earth besides You **(Psalm 73:25)**

Diming your light or playing small to make others feel comfortable benefits no one. Be the light without reservation.

_____

_____

_____

_____

_____

_____

_____

_____

_____

_____

_____

_____

_____

_____

_____

_____

_____

_____

My soul yearns, yes, even pines and is homesick for the courts of the Lord; my heart and my flesh cry out and sing for joy to the living God. **(Psalm 84:2)**

What if, just what if you were WHOLE. What if, just what if you were ENOUGH. What if, just what if there was NOTHING MISSING. Until we get to this point right here there is NO PEACE.

_____

_____

_____

_____

_____

_____

_____

_____

_____

_____

_____

_____

_____

_____

_____

_____

_____

_____

_____

_____

_____

_____

_____

Behold, I long for Your precepts; in Your righteousness give me renewed life **(Psalm 119:40)**